CAMBRIDGE LIBRARY COLLECTION

Books of enduring scholarly value

Maritime Exploration

This series includes accounts, by eye-witnesses and contemporaries, of voyages by Europeans to the Americas, Asia, Australasia and the Pacific during the colonial period. Driven by the military and commercial interests of powers including Britain, France and the Netherlands, particularly the East India Companies, these expeditions brought back a wealth of information on climate, natural resources, topography, and distant civilisations. Their detailed observations provide fascinating historical data for climatologists, ecologists and anthropologists, and the accounts of the mariners' experiences on their long and dangerous voyages are full of human interest.

An Account of a Voyage in Search of La Pérouse

Following the mysterious disappearance of the La Pérouse expedition after it sailed out of Botany Bay in 1788, the French botanist Jacques-Julien Houtou de Labillardière (1755–1834) took part in the search that departed in 1791 from Brest in two ships, *Recherche* and *Espérance*. In the space of three years, the expedition's naturalists collected numerous specimens, with Labillardière focusing on Australian flora, but their missing countrymen were never found. Notwithstanding the later confiscation of the scientific collections by the British – Sir Joseph Banks helped to secure their return – Labillardière was able to publish this narrative to great acclaim in 1800. Reissued here is the English translation of the same year, complete with a volume of finely engraved plates. The work is especially notable for its descriptions and illustrations of the indigenous peoples of Australasia. This volume of illustrations contains more than forty plates depicting people, artefacts, plants and animals.

An Account of a Voyage in Search of La Pérouse

Undertaken by Order of the Constituent Assembly of France,
and Performed in the Years 1791, 1792, and 1793

VOLUME 3: PLATES

JACQUES-JULIEN HOUTOU DE LABILLARDIÈRE

CAMBRIDGE
UNIVERSITY PRESS

CAMBRIDGE
UNIVERSITY PRESS

University Printing House, Cambridge, CB2 8BS, United Kingdom

Cambridge University Press is part of the University of Cambridge.

It furthers the University's mission by disseminating knowledge in the pursuit of
education, learning and research at the highest international levels of excellence.

www.cambridge.org
Information on this title: www.cambridge.org/9781108073776

© in this compilation Cambridge University Press 2014

This edition first published 1800
This digitally printed version 2014

ISBN 978-1-108-07377-6 Paperback

This book reproduces the text of the original edition. The content and language reflect
the beliefs, practices and terminology of their time, and have not been updated.

Cambridge University Press wishes to make clear that the book, unless originally published
by Cambridge, is not being republished by, in association or collaboration with,
or with the endorsement or approval of, the original publisher or its successors in title.

AN ACCOUNT

OF

A VOYAGE

IN SEARCH OF

LA PÉROUSE,

UNDERTAKEN BY ORDER OF THE

CONSTITUENT ASSEMBLY OF FRANCE,

AND PERFORMED

IN THE YEARS 1791, 1792, AND 1793,

IN THE

Recherche and Espérance, Ships of War,

UNDER THE COMMAND OF

REAR-ADMIRAL BRUNI D'ENTRECASTEAUA

TRANSLATED FROM THE FRENCH OF

M. LABILLADIÈRE,

Correspondent of the *ci-devant* Academy of Sciences, Member of the Society of
Natural History of Paris, and
One of the Naturalists attached to the Expedition.

IN TWO VOLUMES OCTAVO.

*With a large Chart, 2 Feet 5 by 20½ Inches, exhibiting the Track of the
Ships ; and 43 other elegant Engravings.*

COLLECTION OF THE PLATES.

LONDON:

PRINTED FOR J. DEBRETT, PICCADILLY.

1800.

Printed by S. Gosnell,
Little Queen Street, Holborn.

LIST OF THE PLATES;

WITH THE PAGES IN THE OCTAVO VOLUMES TO WHICH THEY REFER.

Fig.

N. B. *The articles marked thus * are not referred to in any particular page of the work.
Thofe however in Plates XXXI. XXXII. and XXXIII. belong to Chapter XII. and
thofe in Plate XXXVIII. to Chapter XIII.*

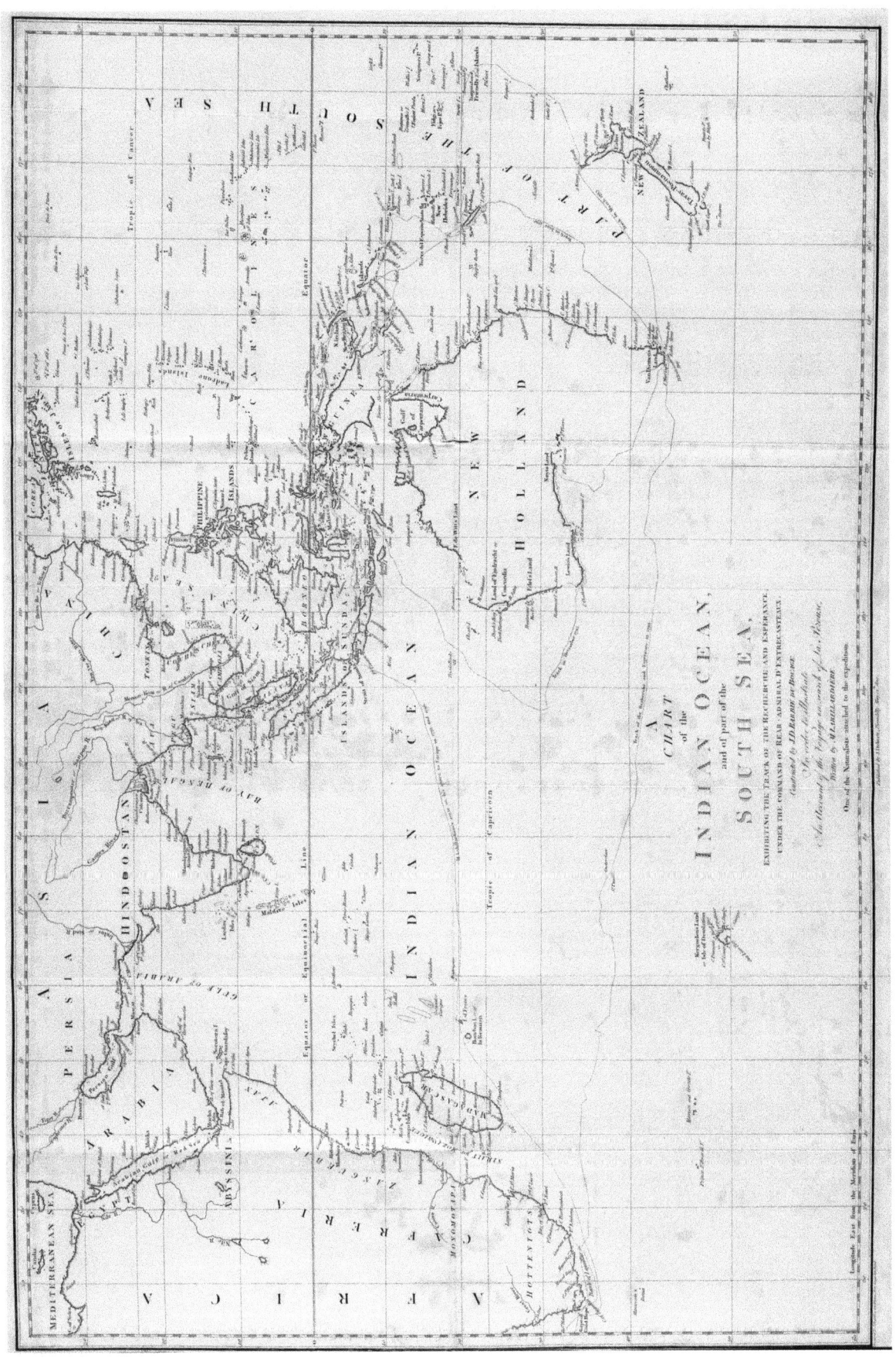

The material originally positioned here is too large for reproduction in this reissue. A PDF can be downloaded from the web address given on page iv of this book, by clicking on 'Resources Available'.

Perm del

Harding sc

Angus sc

VIEW OF THE ADMIRALTY ISLANDS

Published Dec.10 1800 by J. Debrett Piccadilly

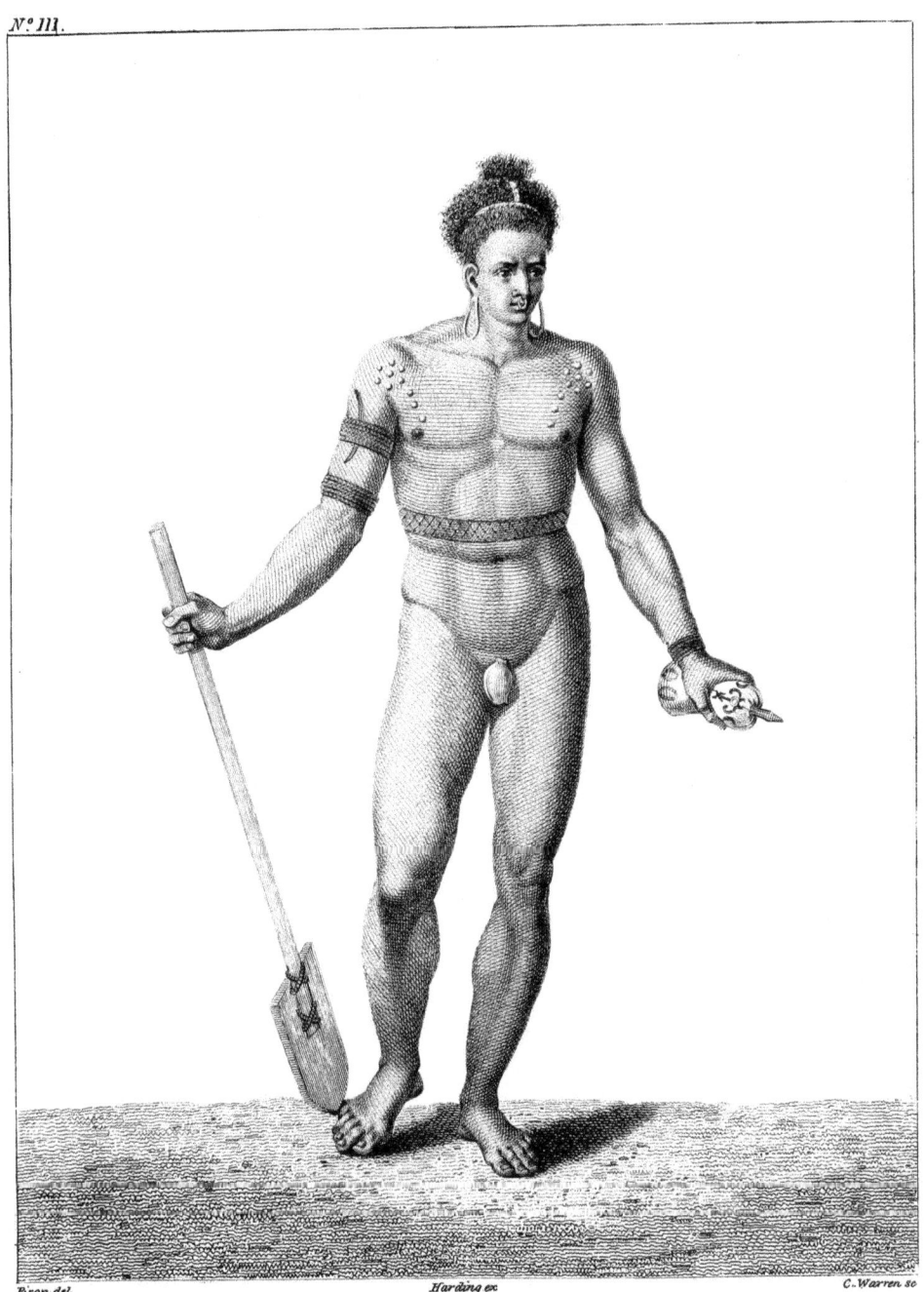

Piron del.   Harding ex.   C. Warren sc

SAVAGE OF THE ADMIRALTY ISLANDS

Pub.ᵈ Apr. 20.1800. by J.Debrett Piccadilly

MANNER OF FISHING OF THE SAVAGES OF CAPE DIEMEN

Peron del.

Harding sc

AW. Warren.sc

SAVAGES OF CAPE DIEMEN PREPARING THEIR MEAL

Peron del.

Hardinges

I Walker sc.

Pub.ᵈ Apr·ᵗ 0.1800 by J.Debrett Piccadilly

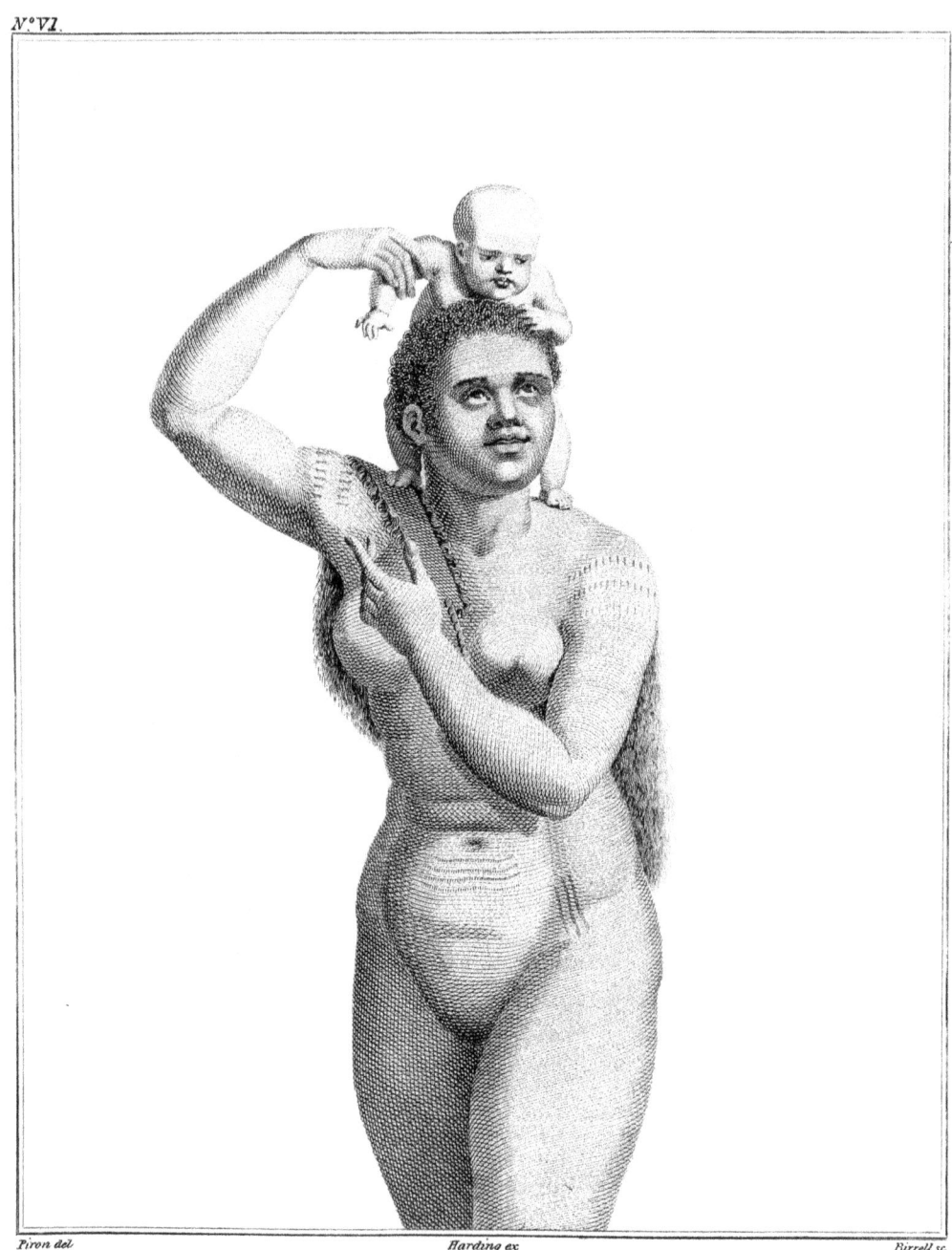

Piron del.   Harding ex.   Birrell sc.

WOMAN OF CAPE DIEMEN

Pub.ᵈ Apr. 20. 1800. by J. Debrett Piccadilly

N°. VII.

Fig. 2.

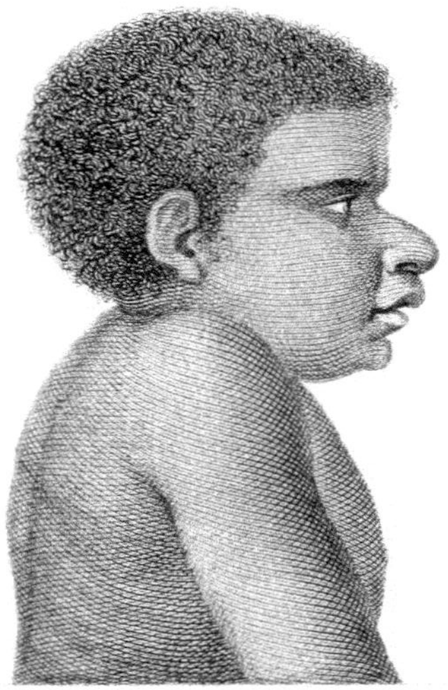

Fig. 1.

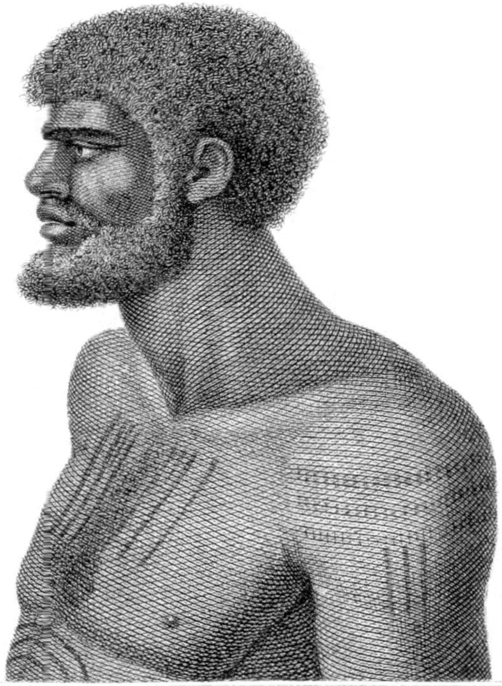

Prion del. Harding ex. Warren sc

BOY of CAPE DIEMEN

MAN of CAPE DIEMEN

Pub: Apr 20. 1800. by. J Debrett Piccadilly

Péron, del.

Harding sc.

Alw. Warren sc.

FEENOU CHIEF OF THE WARRIORS OF TONGATABOO

MAN OF CAPE DIEMEN

Pub.^d Apr. 20 1800 by J.Debrett Piccadilly

Prion. del.

Harding ex.

Eaglqate sc

BLACK SWAN of CAPE DIEMEN

Audebert del.

Harding sc

Eastgate sc

BLACK SPOTTED PARRAKEET OF CAPE DIEMEN

Audebert del.   Harding ex.   Eastgate sc.

CALOA OF THE ISLAND OF WAIGIOU

Publish'd 20 Apr. 1800 by J. Debrett Piccadilly

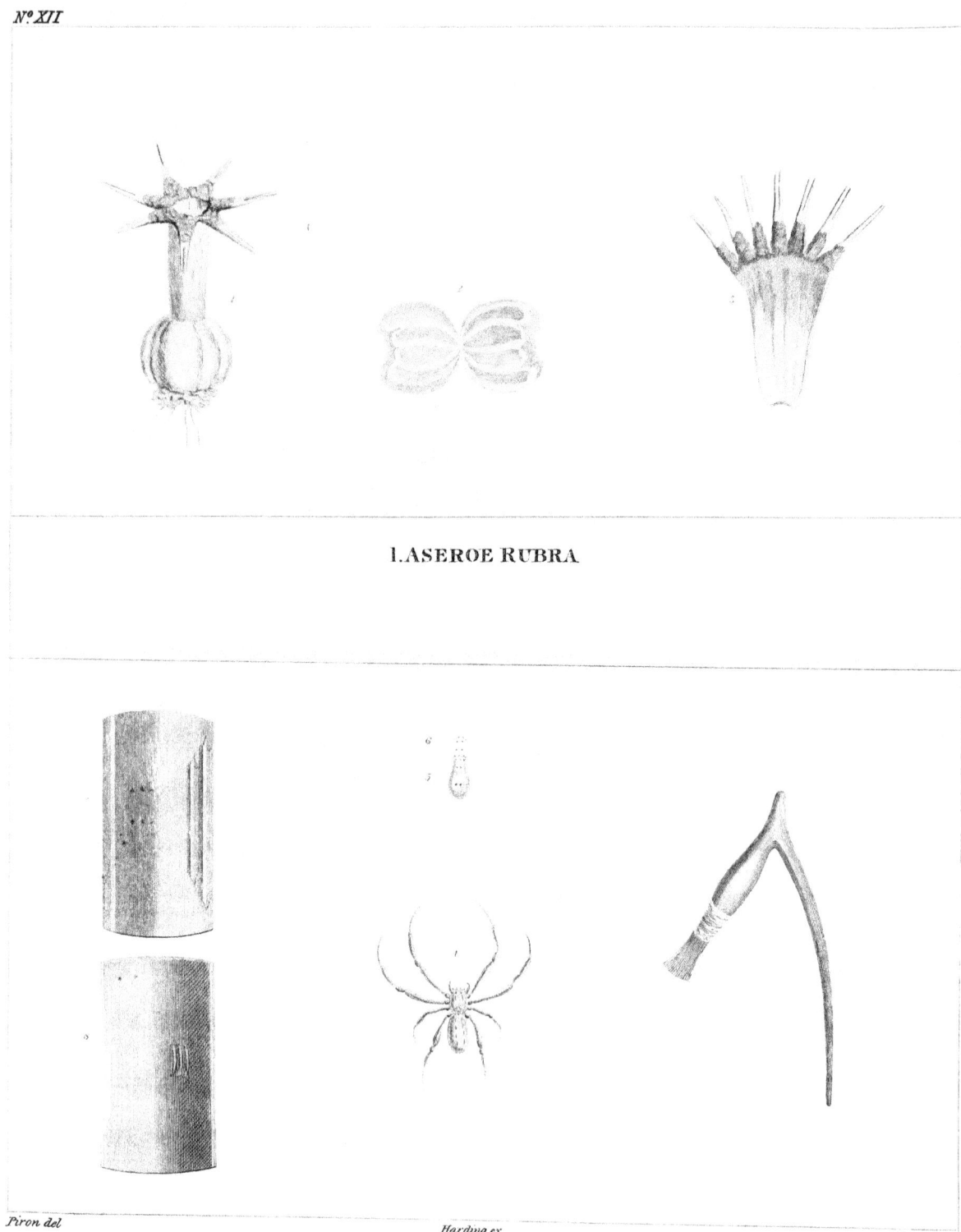

1.ASEROE RUBRA

Piron del   *Harding ex*   *Sparrow sc.*

4 A SPIDER which the **NEW CALEDONIANS EAT .**

Publijhd 20.Apr.1800.by J.Debrett Piccadilly

P.J.Redouté del   Harding sc.   Warren sc

EUCALYPTUS GLOBULUS

Publish'd 20. Apr:1800 by J.Debrett Piccadilly

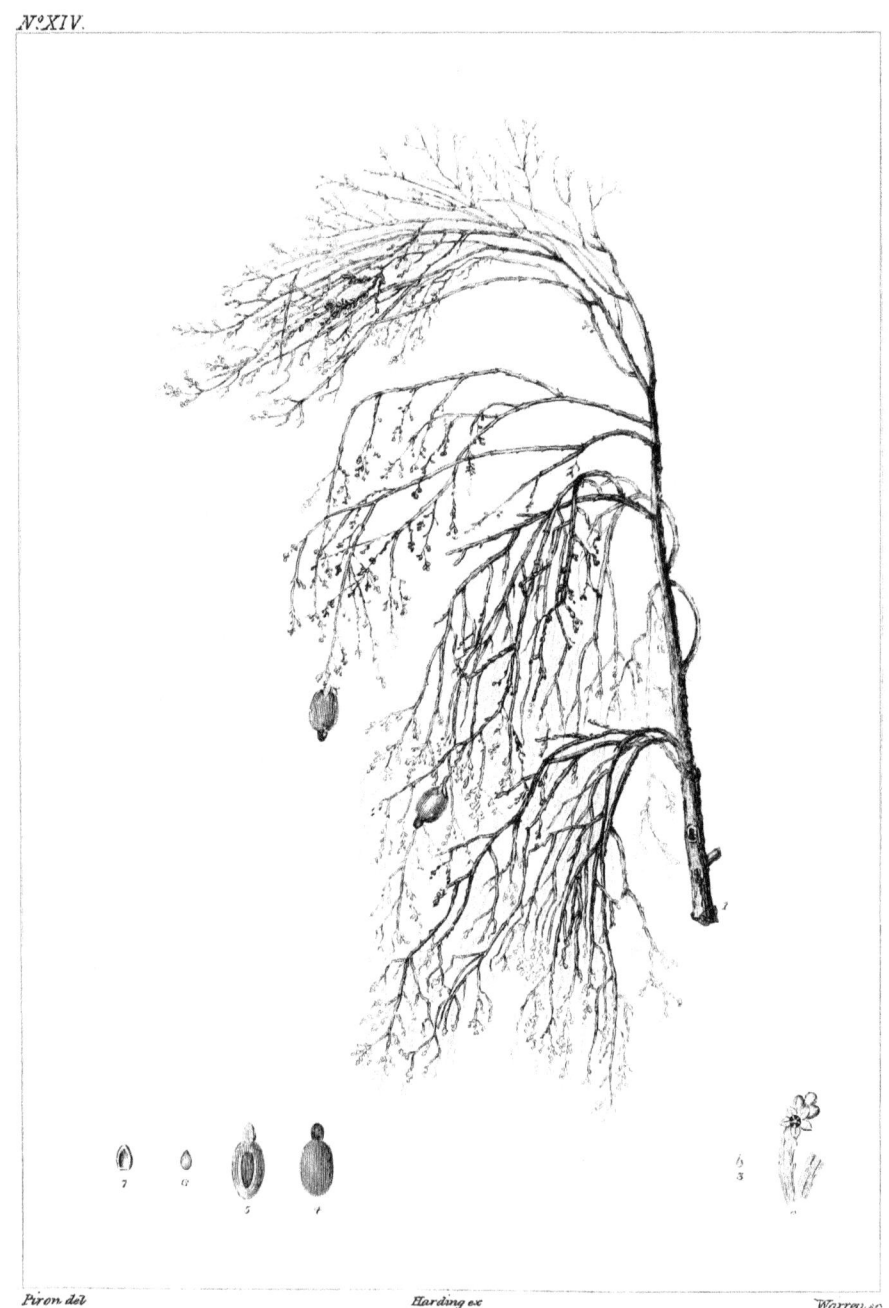

Piron. del.   Harding ex   Warren sc.

EXOCARPOS CUPRESSIFORMIS

Pubᵈ. 20.Apr.1800. by J.Debrett Piccadilly

P.I.Redoute del.　　　　　Harding ex　　　　　Warren sc

DIPLARRENA MORŒA

Publish'd Apr. 20.1800 by J.Debrett Piccadilly

Piron del.

Harding ex.

Sparrow sc.

RICHEA GLAUCA

Pubᵈ Apr 20 1800 by J. Debrett Piccadilly

P.J.Redoute del.   Harding ex   Warren sc

MAZEUTOXERON RUFUM

Publifhd 20.Apr. 1800.by J.Debrett Piccadilly

Prion del.   Harding ex.   Warren sc.

CARPODONTOS LUCIDA

Pub. Apr. 20.1800.by J.Debrett Piccadilly

P.J.Redouté del. Harding ex Warren sc

MAZEUTOXERON REFLEXUM

Pub. Apr. 20.1800. by J.Debrett Piccadilly

P.J. Redouté del.   Harding ex.   Warren sc.

EUCALYPTUS CORNUTA

Publifhd Apr 20.1800 by J.Debrett Piccadilly

P.J.Redouté del.　　　　　　　Harding ex.　　　　　　　Sparrow sc.

CHORIZEMA ILICOFOLIA

Publifhd Apr 20.1800.by J.Debrett Piccadilly

P.J.Redouté del.   Harding ex.   Warren sc.

ANIGOZANTHOS RUFA

Publifhd.20.Apr.1800.by.J.Debrett Piccadilly

P.J.Ridout del.   Harding ex   Warren sc.

BANKSIA REPENS

Publiſhd Apr. 20. 1800. by. J.Debrett. Picadilly

PJ.Redoute del

Harding ex

Sparrow sc.

BANKSIA NIVEA

Publiſhd Apr. 20. 1800. by J.Debrett Piccadilly

Piron del.

Harding sc.

A YOUNG FEMALE SAVAGE OF NEW ZEALAND

Pubᵈ 20 Aprᵗ 1800 by J.Debrett Piccadilly

Warren sc

A SAVAGE OF NEW ZEALAND

Piron del

Harding ex

ENTERTAINMENT GIVEN TO ADMIRAL D'ENTRECASTEAUX

Pub. Apr. 20. 1800.

Eaftgate sc

BY TOOBOU KING OF THE FRIENDLY ISLANDS

.by J.Debrett Piccadilly

Peron del.

Harding sc.

Burrell sc.

A DANCE AT THE FRIENDLY ISLANDS IN PRESENCE OF QUEEN TINEH

DOUBLE CANOE OF THE FRIENDLY ISLANDS

Bryon del.

Harding ex.

Taylor sc.

Perm del

Harding ex

A.W. Warren sc

TOOBOU SON OF THE KING OF THE FRIENDLY ISLANDS

VOUACECEE AN INHABITANT OF FIDGI OR FEJEE

Publish.d.Apr 20 1800 by J.Debrett. Piccadilly

Peron del.

Harding ex

C. Warren sc

WOMAN OF AMBOYNA

WOMAN OF TONGATABOO

Pub. 20 Apr. 1800 by I.Debrett Piccadilly

Harding ex.   Harding sc

ARTICLES IN USE AMONG THE INHABITANTS OF THE FRIENDLY ISLANDS

Pubᵈ Apr. 20, 1800, by J Debrett Piccadilly

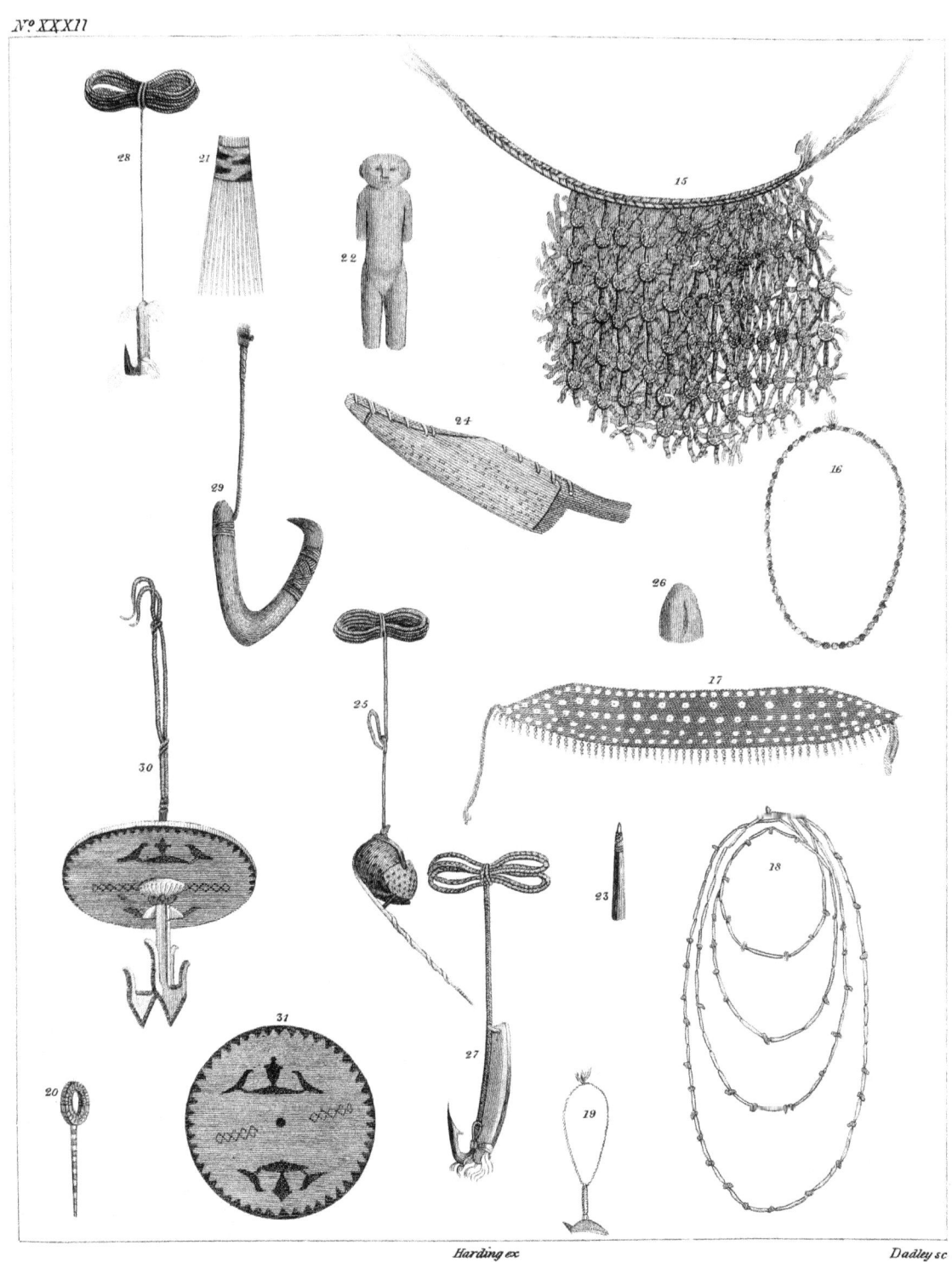

Harding ex   Dadley sc

ARTICLES IN USE AMONG THE INHABITANTS OF THE FRIENDLY ISLANDS

Publish'd 20 Apr.1800.by J.Debrett Piccadilly

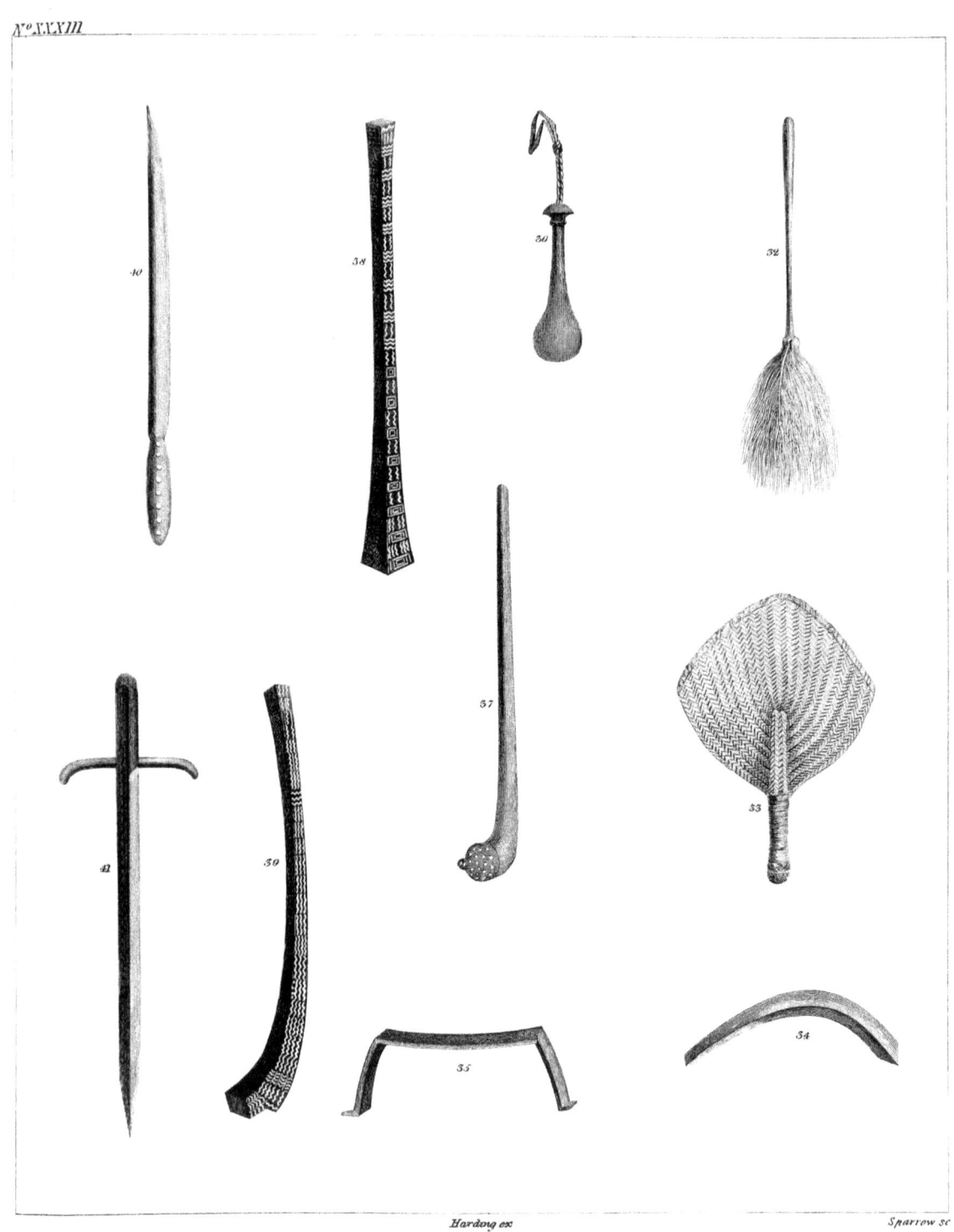

Hardong ex.

Sparrow sc.

ARTICLES IN USE AMONG THE INHABITANTS OF THE FRIENDLY ISLANDS

Publifhd Apr 20. 1800. by J. Debrett, Piccadilly

Fig. 2.

Fig.1.

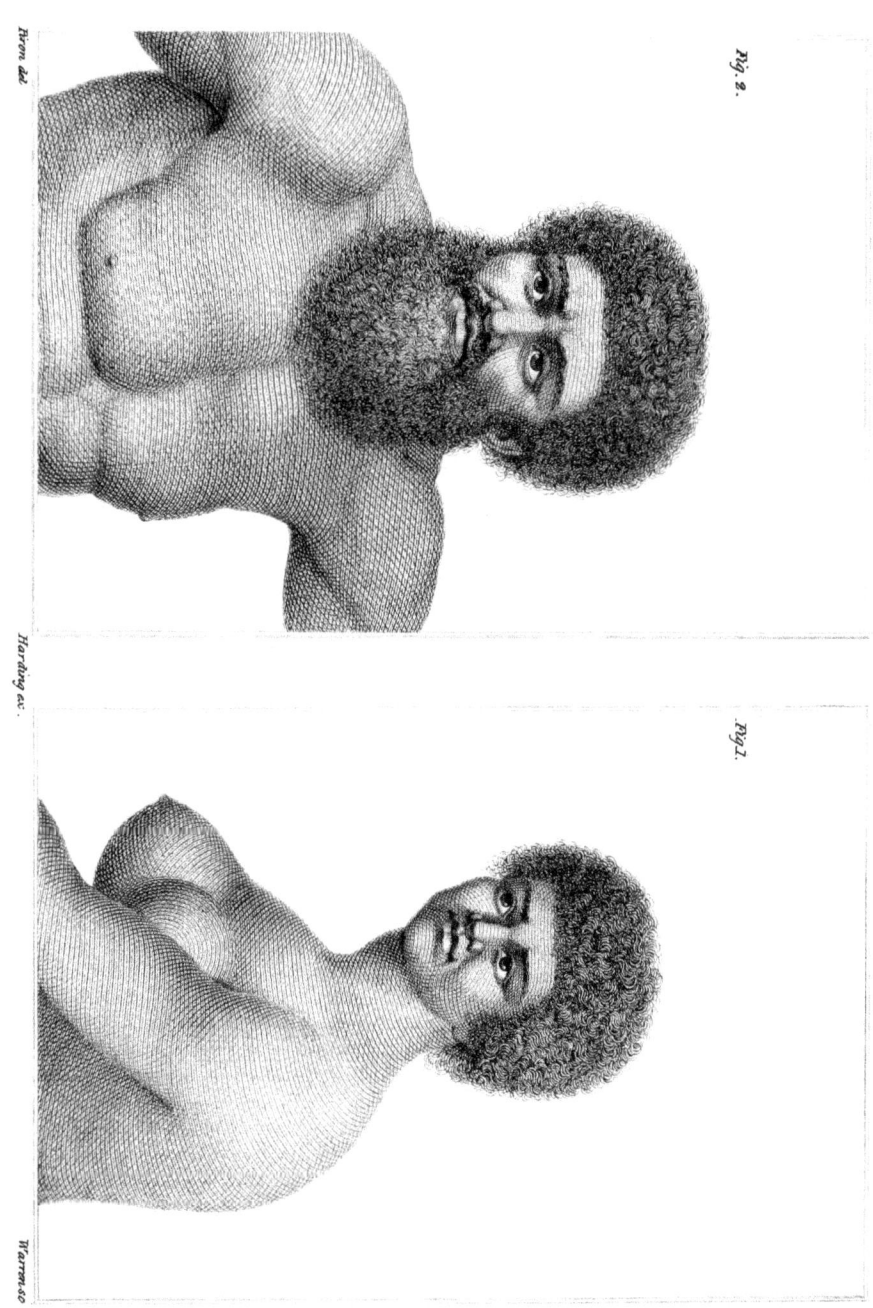

Hirm. del.

Harding sc.

Warren. sc.

MAN OF L'ISLE DE BEAUPRÉ

WOMAN OF L'ISLE DE BEAUPRÉ

Pub.d Apr.t 10.1800. by J.Debrett. Piccadilly.

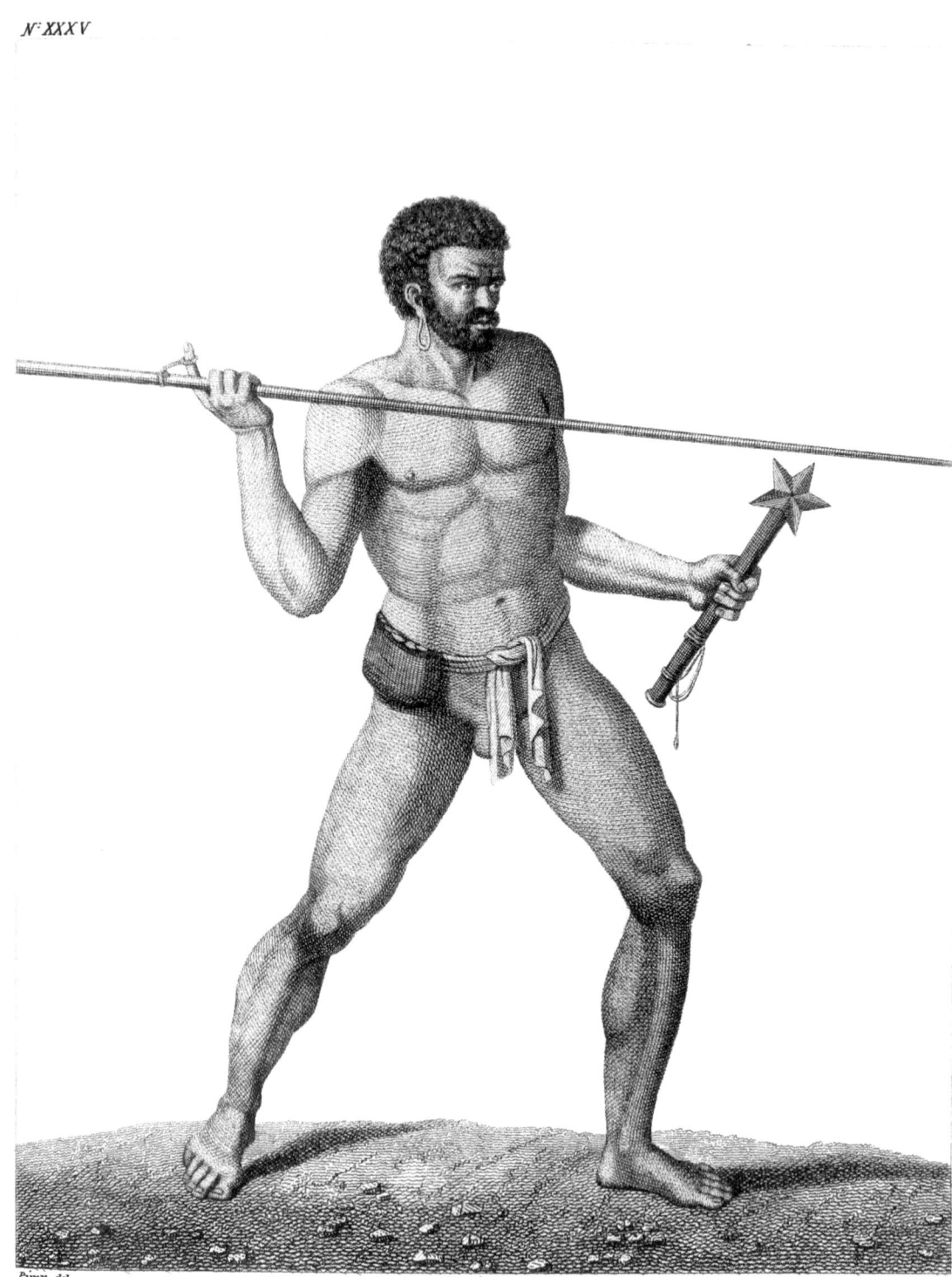

Piron del.   Harding ex.

A SAVAGE OF NEW CALEDONIA THROWING A DART

Pub.ᵈ Apr. 20 1800. by J. Debrett. Piccadilly.

Piron del.   Harding ex

WOMAN OF NEW CALEDONIA

Pub.ᵈ Apr 20.1800.by J.Debrett Piccadilly

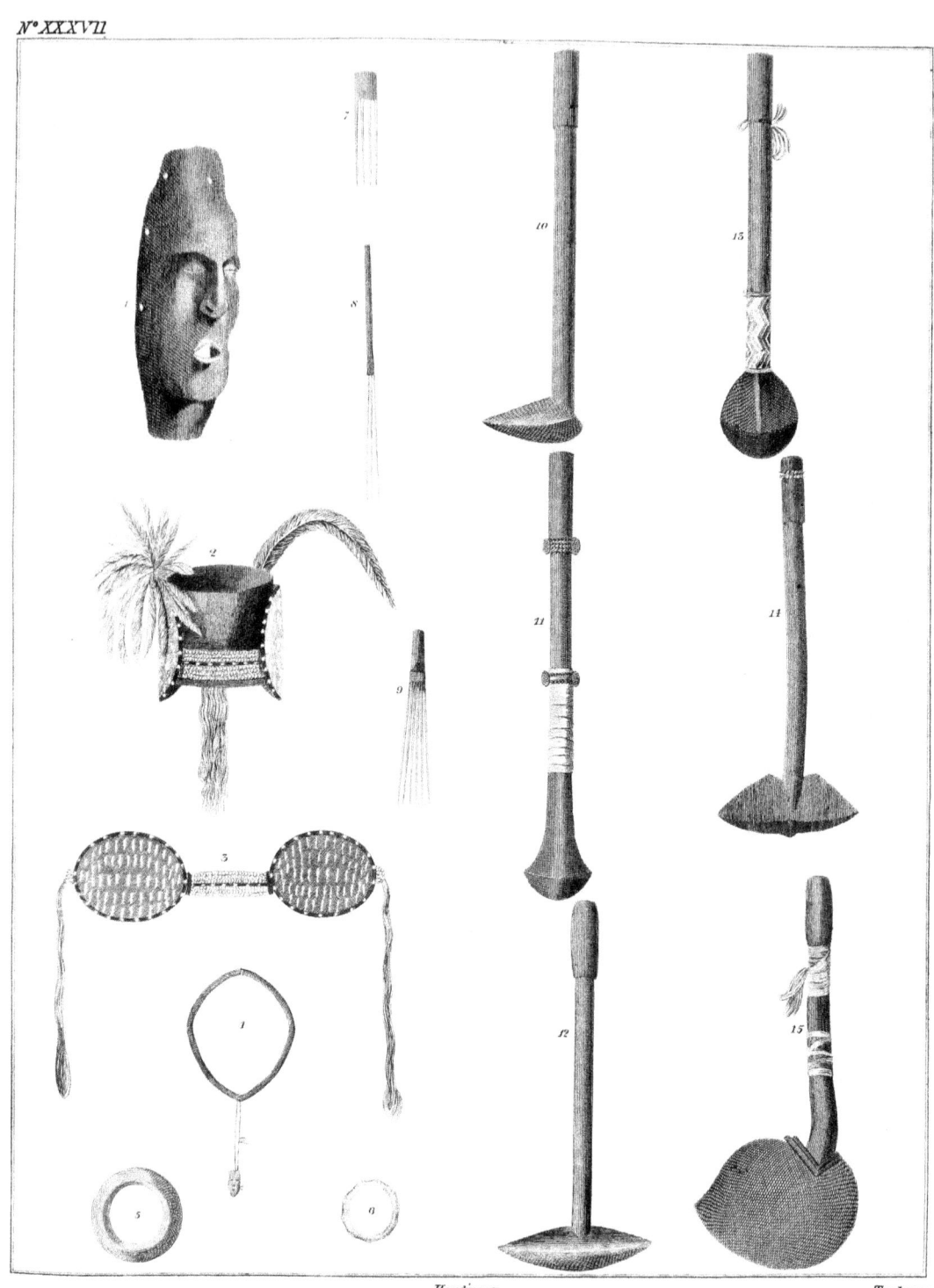

Harding ex.

Taylor sc.

ARTICLES IN USE AMONG THE SAVAGES OF NEW CALEDONIA

Pub.ᵈ 20 Apr. 1800 by J. Debrett Piccadilly

VARIOUS ARTICLES IN USE AMONG THE SAVAGES OF NEW CALEDONIA

HUTS OF THE SAVAGES OF NEW CALEDONIA

Labillardiere del.

Harding ex

Dadley sc.

Publifhd 20.Apr.1800.by J.Debrett Piccadilly

Aubelet del.

Harding sc.

Bantres sc.

MAGPIE OF NEW CALEDONIA

Published 20 Apr: 1800 by J.Debrett, Piccadilly

Piron del.   Harding ex   Warren sc.

DRACOPHYLLUM VERTICILLATUM

Pub. 20 Apr 1800. by J.Debrett. Piccadilly

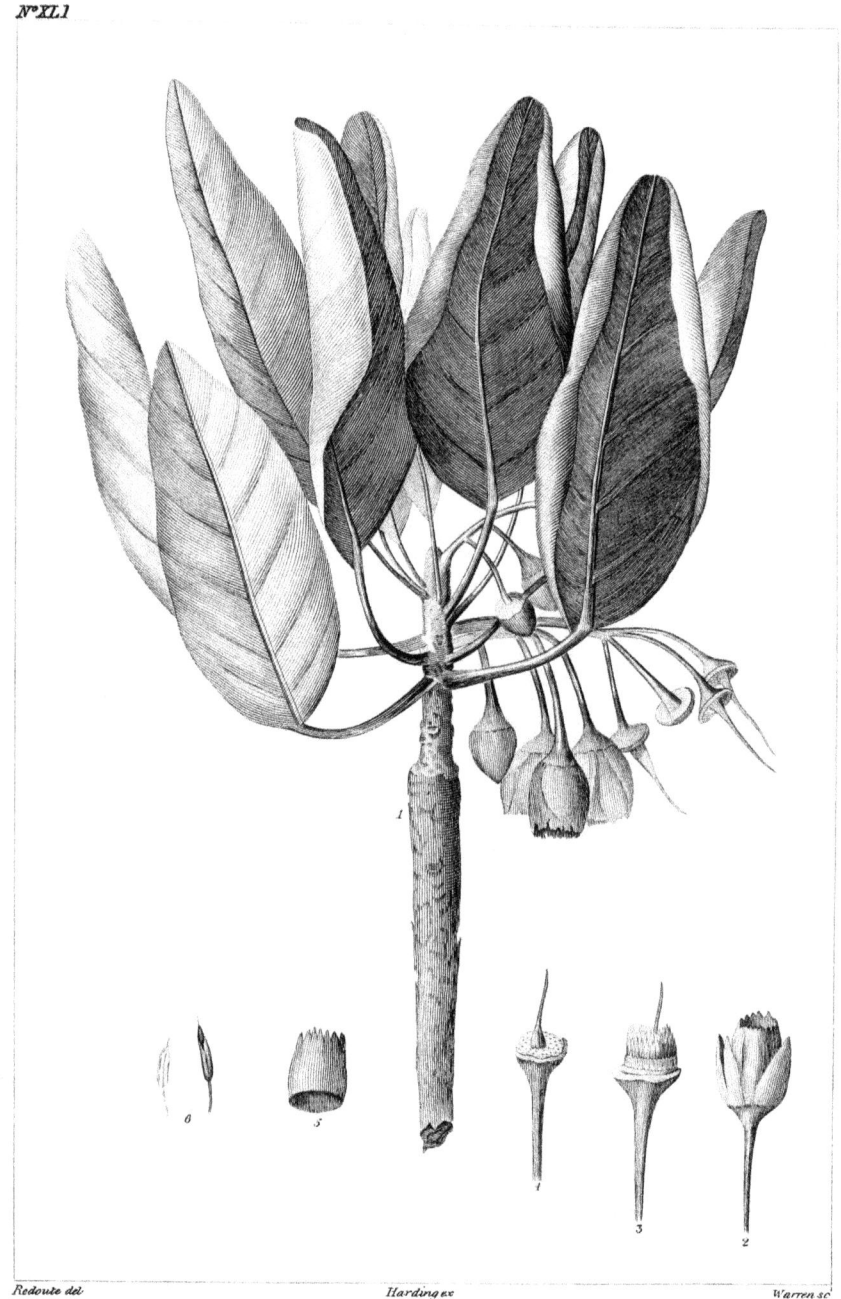

Redouté del.   Harding ex.   Warren sc.

ANTHOLOMA MONTANA

Publiſhd Apr. 20. 1800 by J. Debrett Piccadilly

Ferrn. delt.

Harding sc

W. Angus sc

VIEW IN THE ISLAND OF BOURO TAKEN FROM THE ROADSTEAD

Publish'd Apr 20,1800. by J.Debrett Piccadilly

CANOE OF THE ISLAND OF BOUKA

Piron del   Harding ex   Warren sc

CANOE OF THE ARSACIDES

Publishᵈ Apr. 20. 1800 by J. Debrett Piccadilly

A Double Canoe of New Caledonia

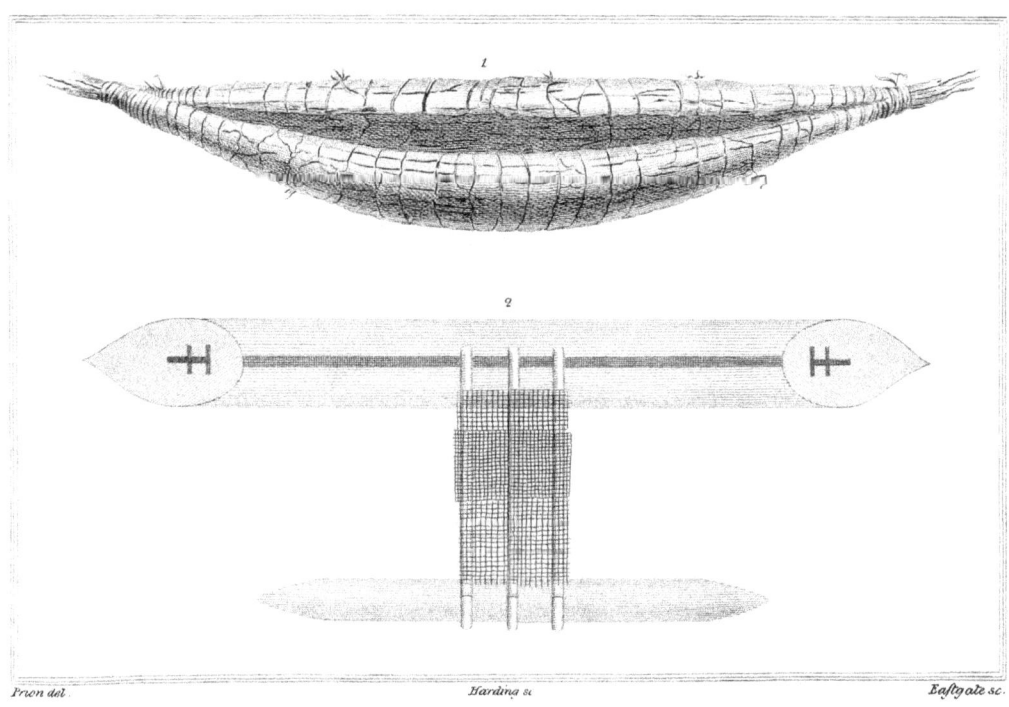

Prion del.   Harding sc   Eastgate sc.

1. A CATAMARAN OF CAPE DIEMEN. 2. A CANOE OF SANTA CRUZ OR EGMONT ISLAND

Publifhd Apr. 20.1800. by J.Debrett. Piccadilly

For EU product safety concerns, contact us at Calle de José Abascal, 56–1°, 28003 Madrid, Spain or eugpsr@cambridge.org.

www.ingramcontent.com/pod-product-compliance
Ingram Content Group UK Ltd.
Pitfield, Milton Keynes, MK11 3LW, UK
UKHW051425240426
470322UK00020B/624